COLOR TIPS

As a designer, I love to experiment with colors and to mix techniques and mediums. For me, bright and bold always looks good. Sometimes I like all warm colors and sometimes all cool colors. Other times I randomly mix warm and cool colors together in the same design, creating a bold complementary palette. Check out the handy color wheel below. Each color is labeled with a P (primary), S (secondary), or T (tertiary). In the very center of the wheel, you'll see a circle of lighter colors, called tints. A tint is a color plus white. On the outer edges of the wheel, you'll see a ring of darker colors, called shades. A shade is a color plus black. The colors on the top half of the color wheel are considered warm colors (red, yellow, and orange), and the colors on the bottom half are called cool (green, blue, and purple). Colors opposite one another on the color wheel are called complementary, and colors that are next to each other are called analogous. Experiment with color yourself with this quick reference page to serve as inspiration!

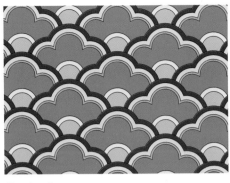

Cool colors

Warm colors

A mix of cool and warm colors

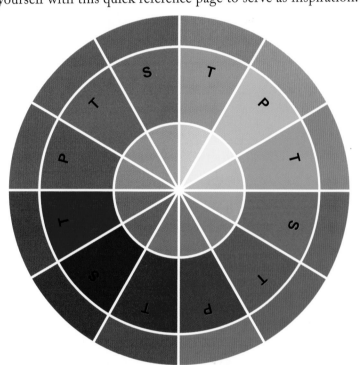

Primary colors: The primary colors are red, yellow, and blue. They are called "primary" because they can't be created by mixing other colors.

Secondary colors: Mixing primary colors together creates the secondary colors orange, green, and purple (violet).

Tertiary colors: Mixing a primary color and a secondary color together creates the tertiary colors yellow-orange, yellow-green, blue-green, blue-purple, red-purple, and red-orange.

1

COLOR IDEAS

Patterns within patterns can be made by repeating sets of colors in repeating designs. For example, if the same motif is repeated within one design, you can approach the coloring in different ways. Check out the samples on this page for ideas.

Remember, there are no right or wrong ways to color these designs. This book was created for your enjoyment. As you are coloring, take your time, relax, and enjoy the creative and meditative experience. Each page is filled with details and forms you can choose to color in a variety of ways. Try a bright and bold color palette with solids on one page, then try a soft, pastel scheme with shading and gradients on another page. You will be amazed at the variety of results!

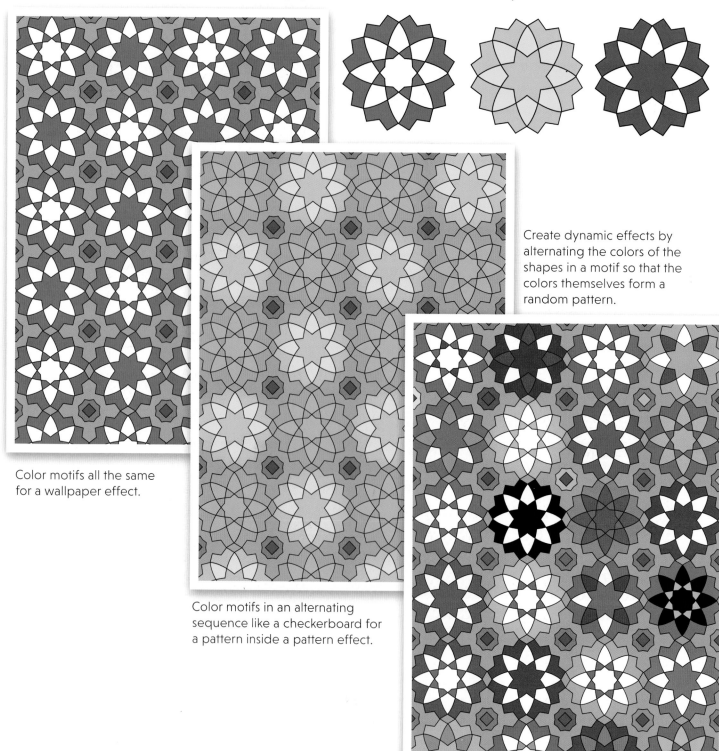

Create dynamic effects by alternating the colors of the shapes in a motif so that the colors themselves form a random pattern.

Color motifs all the same for a wallpaper effect.

Color motifs in an alternating sequence like a checkerboard for a pattern inside a pattern effect.

Color Layering

As shown in the design below, it is best to start with the lightest colors first—in this case, purple and orange. Then add a darker color, such as the red shown. In this color sample, the next step is to add some nice contrasting green elements. As a last step, you can add a color to the background. Feel free to add gradations to your color fills for a softer look or use all solid color fills for a bolder effect.

COLOR INSPIRATION

The following pages are filled with colored samples to get you thinking and imagining. First, you'll find pages full of multiple color ideas for single images, so you can see how a different color scheme and approach can make the same design look radically different. Then, you'll find several gorgeous hand-colored pieces using a variety of different art mediums by the talented artist Marie Browning. Enjoy the colorful inspiration here before you sit down to create beautiful art yourself—let your creativity flow!

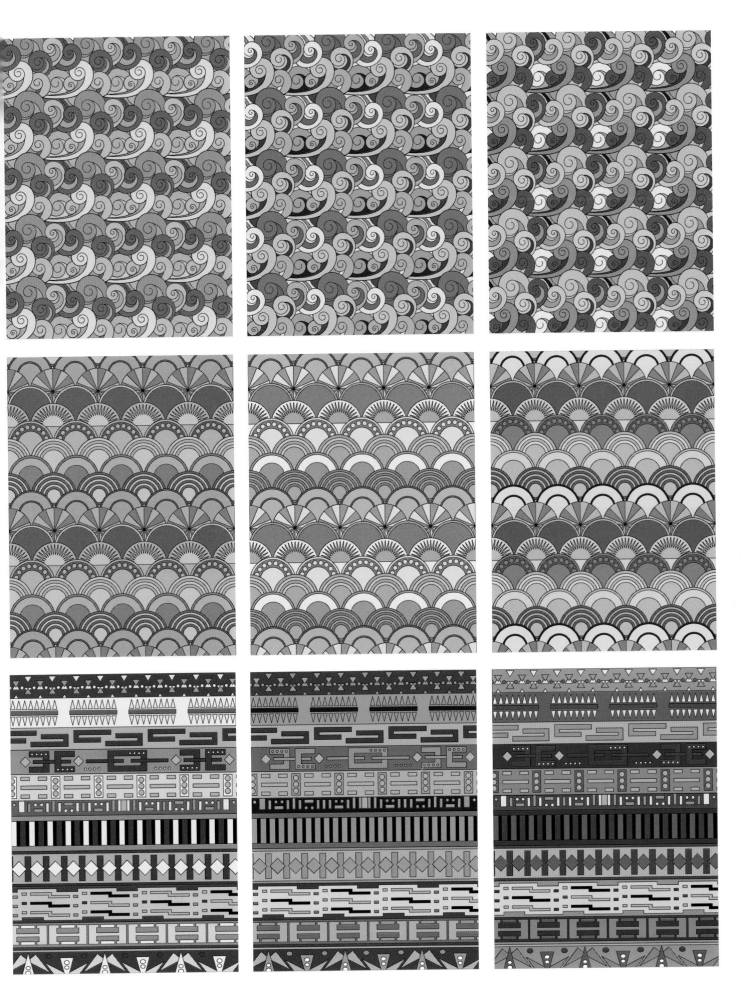

Irojiten Colored Pencils (Tombow), Gel Pens (Sakura). Rich Tones. Color by Marie Browning.

Pitt Pastel Pencils (Faber-Castell), Gel Pens (Sakura). Muted Tones. Color by Marie Browning.

Dual Brush Markers (Tombow), Gel Pens (Sakura). Monochromatic Tones. Color by Marie Browning.

Irojiten Colored Pencils (Tombow), Gel Pens (Sakura). Southwest Tones. Color by Marie Browning.

Dual Brush Markers (Tombow). Modern Tones. Color by Marie Browning.

Dual Brush Markers (Tombow), Gel Pens (Sakura). Sea Tones. Color by Marie Browning.

Dual Brush Markers (Tombow). Designer Tones. Color by Marie Browning.

Don't you know how sweet and
wonderful life can be?

—Marvin Gaye

How wonderful it is that nobody
need wait a single moment before
starting to improve the world.

—Anne Frank

It is not in the stars to hold our
destiny but in ourselves.

—WILLIAM SHAKESPEARE, *Julius Caesar*

Life is like riding a bicycle.
To keep your balance, you must
keep moving.

—UNKNOWN

Happiness is part of who we are.
Joy is the feeling.

—Tony DeLiso

They say a person needs just three things to be truly happy in this world: someone to love, something to do, and something to hope for.

—Tom Bodett

And above all, watch with glittering eyes the whole world around you, because the greatest secrets are always hidden in the most unlikely places.

—ROALD DAHL, *The Minpins*

Happiness is when what you
think, what you say, and what you
do are in harmony.

—Mahatma Gandhi

Every mountaintop is within
reach if you just keep climbing.

—Unknown

Yesterday is gone. Tomorrow has
not yet come. We have only today.
Let us begin.

—Mother Teresa

It is good to have an end to
journey toward; but it is the
journey that matters,
in the end.

—Ernest Hemingway

If you cannot find peace within
yourself, you will never find it
anywhere else.

—MARVIN GAYE

A day without laughter
is a day wasted.

—Nicolas Chamfort

We do not need magic to transform our world. We carry all the power we need inside ourselves already.

—J.K. ROWLING

I can choose either to be a victim
of the world or an adventurer
in search of treasure. It's all a
question of how I view my life.

—Paulo Coelho, *Eleven Minutes*

The world seemed to shimmer a
little at the edges.

—Neil Gaiman, *Coraline*

49

Count your age by friends,
not years. Count your life by
smiles, not tears.

—Unknown

Don't be afraid of your fears.
They're not there to scare you.
They're there to let you know that
something is worth it.

—C. JoyBell C.

53

You must give everything to make your life as beautiful as the dreams that dance in your imagination.

—ROMAN PAYNE

When we love, we always strive
to become better than we are.
When we strive to become better
than we are, everything around us
becomes better too.

—PAUL COELHO, *The Alchemist*

Think big thoughts but relish
small pleasures.

—H. Jackson Brown Jr.

Happiness doesn't have to
be chased… it merely has
to be chosen.

—Mandy Hale

There's nowhere you can be that
isn't where you're meant to be.

—THE BEATLES, *All You Need Is Love*

Sometimes the dreams that come
true are the dreams you never
even knew you had.

—Alice Sebold, *The Lovely Bones*

Life isn't about finding yourself.
Life is about creating yourself.

—GEORGE BERNARD SHAW

Do not spoil what you have by desiring what you have not.

—Epicurus

I know not all that may be
coming, but be it what it will,
I'll go to it laughing.

—HERMAN MELVILLE, *Moby-Dick*

Everything changes but
beauty remains.

—Kelly Clarkson, *A Moment Like This*